First Phrases from Around the World

Everyday Arabic

Tricia Hoffman

Little Mitchie
an imprint of Mitchell Lane

CREATING YOUNG NONFICTION READERS

Little Mitchie books spark curiosity and support early nonfiction reading for students in Grades 2-3. Designed to build vocabulary, support second language learners, and prepare readers for middle-grade content, each book includes helpful tips for parents and educators to build confidence and deepen understanding of the world.

TIPS FOR READING NONFICTION WITH BEGINNING READERS

Talk about Nonfiction

Begin by explaining that nonfiction books give us information that is true. The book will be organized around a specific topic or idea, and we may learn new facts through reading.

Look at the Parts

Most nonfiction books have helpful features. Our *Little Mitchie* titles include color photographs and graphic aids, a table of contents, a glossary, and an index. Share the purpose of these features with your reader.

Color Photos and Graphic Aids

A lot of information can be found by "reading" photos, charts, maps, and other graphic aids found within nonfiction texts. Help your reader learn more about the different ways information can be displayed.

Table of Contents

Located at the front of the book, this list shows the big ideas within the text and the page numbers where they can be found.

Index

Located at the back of the book, an index is an alphabetical list of topics and the page numbers where they can be found.

With a little help and guidance about reading nonfiction, you can feel good about introducing a young reader to the world of *Little Mitchie* nonfiction books.

Little Mitchie is an imprint of:

Mitchell Lane
PUBLISHERS

2001 SW 31st Avenue
Hallandale, FL 33009
mitchelllanepub.com

First Edition, 2027.

Author: Tricia Hoffman
Designer: Kathy Walsh
Editor: Tricia Hoffman

Library of Congress Cataloging-in-Publication Data
Title: Everyday Arabic / by Tricia Hoffman

Description: Hallandale, FL :
Mitchell Lane Publishers, [2027]

Identifiers:
Library bound ISBN: 979-8-89260-908-1
Paperback ISBN: 979-8-90145-059-8
eBook ISBN: 979-8-90145-018-5

Library of Congress Control Number: 2026930171

PHOTO CREDITS: Cover and Title pg: iukhym_vova, smile3377; Doodle Art: devitaayu, FourLeafLover, wanchana, veekicl, Rizky, mhatzapa, Kebon doodle, Asyam Design, piixypeach, syoko: istock: background, rica nohara; p 4, Ami Parikh, ViDI Studio, aleks333; p 5, PixelsMD Production; p 6, Jelena Stanojkovic, oneinchpunch; p 7, Eric Isselee, zurijeta; p 9, SCHAMIN; p 10, soumen82hazra, peopleImages, Denys Kurbatov; p 11, Zurijeta; p 12, shablovskyistock, pics fives, chiociolla, BongoStock, diplomedia; p 13, Bet_Noire, 4 PM production, Andrew Angelox, Prostock-studio, Dmytro Zinkevych; p 15, Drazen Zigic, Prostock-studio; p 16, oneinchpunch, Dmytro Zinkevych, ZouZou; p 17, Roman Samborskyi; p 18, NIKS ADS, Andril Lemelianenko, Elaf Alchurbaji; p 19, Pressmaster, Monkey Business Images; p 20, sohailalee, aleks333, Pixel-Shot; p 21, vitals, Esin Deniz; Nataly Studio, suplob_Designer, oneinchpunch, Creativa Images; p 22, Hatthakon, Pixel-Shot, StockimageFactory.com; p 23, Prostock-studio

Table of Contents

This Is Me

eumri thamani sanawatin.

I am eight years old.

asmi fatima.

My name is Fatima.

hadha ‘ana

wahed
one
ithneen
two
thalaatha
three
‘arbaa’a
four
khamsa
five
sitta
six
saba’a
seven
thamaaniya
eight
tisa’a
nine
a’shra
ten

mae alsalamati!
Goodbye!

People and Pets

'aeish mae eayilati.

I live with my family.

'ukht
sister

al'umu
mother

'ab
father

shaqiq
brother

alnaas walhayawanat al'alifa

alkalb
dog

qitta
cat

eusfur
bird

sahalia
lizard

far
mouse

'arnab
rabbit

Today

alyawm hu althulatha'a.

Today is Tuesday.

al'ahad
Sunday

aliathnayn
Monday

althulatha'
Tuesday

al'arbiea'
Wednesday

alkhamis
Thursday

aljumuea
Friday

alsabt
Saturday

alshahr hu 'aghustus.

The month is August.

yanayir.	January
fibrayir.	February
maris	March
'abril.	April
mayw.	May
yuniu	June
yuliu.	July
'aghustus	August
sibtambar	September
'uktubar.	October
nufimbir	November
disambir	December

alyawm

'iinah har fi alkhariji.

It is hot outside.

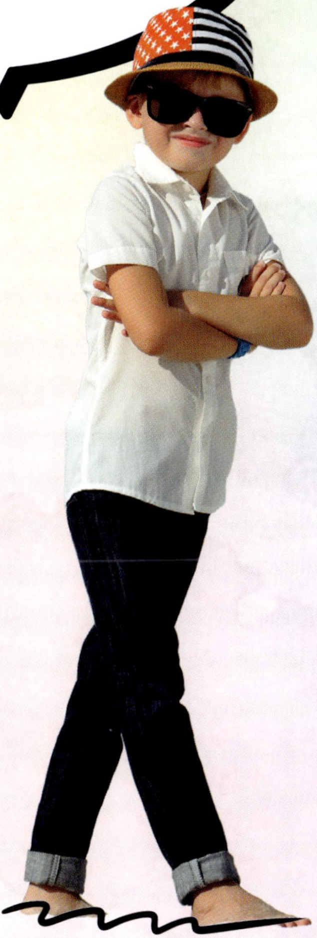

mishmis
sunny

barid
cold

mumtir
rainy

easif
windy

Morning

sabah alkhayri!

Good morning!

'amsht shieri.

I comb my hair.

'aghsal 'asnani.

I brush my teeth.

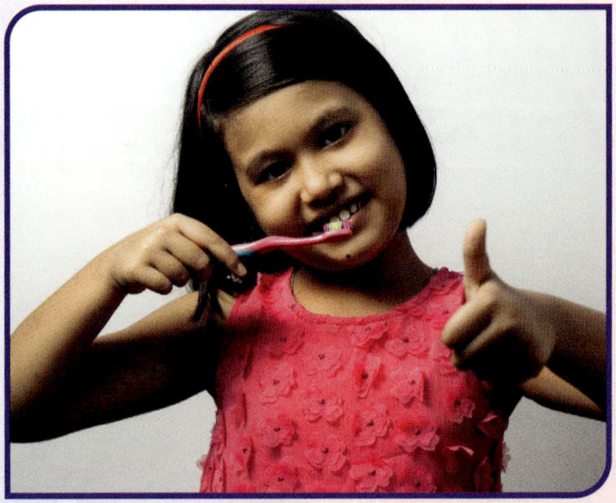

sabah

'artadi qmysan 'ahmaru.

I wear a red shirt.

burtuqali	'asfar	'azraq	'akhdar	
orange	yellow	blue	green	
'arjuani	'ahmar	wardi	'aswad	abyad
purple	red	pink	black	white

Breakfast

'urid hubub al'iiftar, min fadliki.

I want cereal for breakfast, please.

khubz muhamas
toast

easir alburtuqal
orange juice

halibi
milk

bayda
egg

‘iiftar

alhafilat huna.
han waqt aliantilaqi!

The bus is here.
It is time to go!

hafilat madrasia
school bus

haqibat alzuhr
backpack

School

'adhhab 'iilaa almadrasati.

I go to school.

qaratu.

I read.

ana amaris alriyadiaati.

I do math.

madrasa

ana bihajat alaa musaeidatin.

I need help.

mudaris
teacher

maktab
desk

hal li 'an 'adhhab 'iilaa alhamami?

May I go to the bathroom?

Time to Play

hal sataleab maei?

Will you play with me?

naem!

Yes!

'arkudu.
I run.

'ana 'ata'arjahu.
I swing.

waqt allaeib

Neighborhood

'aeish fi hayin sakani.

I live in a neighborhood.

alwwh lisadiqi.

I wave to my friend.

'adhhab 'iilaa almatajari.

I go to the store.

hy

kam taklifat hadha?

How much does this cost?

manzil
house

shajara
tree

alzuhur
flowers

sharie
street

skutar
scooter

eushb
grass

Dinner

hal han waqt aleasha'i?

Is it time for dinner?

niema, min fadlika.
Yes, please.

la, shkraan.
No, thank you.

easha'

'ahibu altaeam alearabii.

I like Arabic food.

hims
hummus

shawarma
shawarma

falafil
falafel

kibbeh
kibbeh

'uhibu altaeam al'amrikii.

I like American food.

himbirghir
hamburger

batatis maqlia
french fries

Night

'artadi bijama.

I wear pajamas.

'ana 'adhhab 'iilaa alfarashi.

I go to bed.

'aghmid eayni.

I close my eyes.

layla

tab masawuk!
Good night!
dimyat dub
teddy bear
wisadatan
pillow

Index

About Arabic

Arabic is the first language of more than 300 million people. Many more people speak Arabic as a second language. It is the fifth most common language in the world. The top five countries where Arabic is spoken are Egypt, Algeria, Sudan, Saudi Arabia, and Morocco. Arabic is the official language of 22 countries in the Middle East, North Africa, and Asia. Arabic is written from right to left, unlike most languages that are written from left to right.